To my family, without whom many of these stories would have never happened.

Trail Tales

A collection of entertaining trail stories

Robert M. Cowdrick

Copyright © 2019 Robert M. Cowdrick
All Rights Reserved

ISBN-13: 978-1-7333613-0-9
ISBN-10: 1-7333613-0-8
Published by: Robert M. Cowdrick
First Edition August 2019

All rights reserved. No part of this book may be reproduced or transmitted in any form or by any means, electronic or mechanical, including photocopying, recording, or by any information storage and retrieval system, without permission in writing from the copyright owner.

This is an original work. Names, characters, places and incidents are the product of the author's imagination or are used fictitiously, and any resemblance to any actual persons, living or dead, events, or locales is entirely coincidental

This book was printed in the United States of America

Contents

Mucking Around In Maine   1

Lost And Found   9

Packers   17

Bridging The Gap   25

¡Hola! ¿Como Estás?   31

Glacier Bound   39

On A Mission   47

Simply Dynamite   51

Cut It Out   57

Come Back At 4:00pm   65

Trail Security   73

Watch Your Step   81

On Top Of It All   91

The Things They Carried   99

Where To From Here   105

Acknowledgements   107

Mucking Around In Maine

I arrived at the Bangor International Airport on a sunny August day. From the baggage claim, I collected my duffle bag and backpack. I nervously searched the crowd for my planned ride to the Maine Appalachian Trail Club's Base Camp.

Unsure of exactly when my ride would arrive, I stepped outside to enjoy the Pine Tree State's summer air. In a few minutes, a dusty white Chevy passenger van pulled up and out jumped Devon and Brandon.

"You must be Bob," Brandon remarked. "Let me take your gear. Jump in. We're heading to downtown Bangor to pick up the rest of the crew," Devon added. "And we want to pick up some items before we head to the woods."

Working as a volunteer for the Maine Appalachian Trail Club was my first experience as a trail crewmember. Maine had been my home for many years and I thought this would be the best place to start my trail building experience. During my college years at the University of Maine, I spent my summer vacations working in the woods as a camp counselor, and later I worked as a seasonal forester for two large paper companies in Maine.

We drove through Bangor passing white clad aging mansions, boutique shops of all kinds and restaurants serving Maine staples such as lobster rolls, whoopie pies and Moxie cola.

At the next stop light, a small group of individuals waved us down. In climbed five others who would complete our crew of eight for the week working along the Appalachian Trail (AT) at Rainbow Lake. "Welcome Bob. You made it" they chimed in, "Glad to have you on our hitch".

Hitch. On our Hitch. A new term to me but excited to be part of this crew. A remarkably talented group of 20 year olds who were searching for what they wanted to do next in life.

Devon was a Canadian history graduate with welcoming personal skills.

Brandon, a talented guitar player from Ohio who could create a tune from scratch.

Noah, a summer environmental intern from Missouri was looking for some resume building experience.

Casey, a Massachusetts Asian studies major thru-hiked the AT two years before and wanted to return to Maine.

Trail Tales 3

Cree, an experienced trail maintainer, spent previous summers in Montana and New Mexico building trails.

Yi, a young female biologist from Maine wanted to get out of the office and see more of the state.

Davie, grew up in western Pennsylvania and loved to be outside hiking in the North Maine Woods

I, the lone senior adult on the hitch filled out the crew of eight.

After collecting the other crewmember's gear from the base camp, Devon turned the van onto Route 15 and we headed north to the woods.

We passed through the iconic Maine towns of Kenduskeag, Corinth, Dover- Foxcroft, Milo and Brownville, all with a deep history of their own. After driving for three hours on bumpy frost heaved roads, we arrived in Millinocket.

Once a thriving paper mill town employing thousands of workers, Millinocket is now a ghost town. Because paper production now is done overseas, the paper mills closed. Attempts to restart the mills have failed and now the revitalization of the town hinges on tourism, hunting and fishing.

We made a quick stop at the Katahdin General Store, a store that has everything you would ever need. Food, clothing, tools, Maine trinkets, nuts, bolts, screws and sweets of all kinds. The crew grabbed a few last minute supplies, mostly ice cream and whoopie pies to hold them over until we returned to civilization in a week, and we were back on the road again.

We turned onto the Golden Road, a 96-mile long private "gravel haul" road stretching from Millinocket to the St. Zacharie

Border Crossing in Canada. Built by the Great Northern Paper Company, the road was primarily used by logging trucks hauling oversize loads of logs to the paper mills.

    As the road noise got louder, the music cranked up with songs from artists with names I did not know and whose songs definitely were not on my personal playlists. Maroon 5 and Imagine Dragons resounded from the speakers. This hitch was not going to be the Billy Joel and Linda Ronstadt genre.

    Brandon cranked up the volume when his favorite songs began and the crew joined in with the lyrics. Nonetheless, they were a welcoming group of young adults and I was excited to be in the North Maine Woods.

Rainbow Lake along the Appalachian Trail in Maine.

At the trailhead, we loaded our packs with food, community gear and tools before heading southbound on the AT to our jobsite. For the next seven days, we were going to build elevated step stone paths, called turnpikes, along the edge of Rainbow Lake.

Rainbow Lake is a pristine body of water that Appalachian Trail hikers pass by on their way out of the 100-mile wilderness and onto Mt. Katahdin. This section of trail, which is on Nature Conservancy land, follows the edge of the lake. Occasionally it runs through marshes and bogs making it a difficult and wet section to traverse.

The Appalachian Trail near Rainbow Lake before adding a turnpike.

Trail Tales

Creating a dry trail through this mucky section involved first quarrying rocks. We spread out along the trail looking for large beach ball size boulders hiding under the leaves, duff and dirt. It was a big game of hide and seek.

The crew worked with rock bars, shovels, Pulaskis, and trail hoes to unearth the hidden gems. Whenever someone found a large boulder, everyone pitched in to help unearth it and then move it.

Carefully we rolled the monster rocks toward the trail and into the muck. It would slowly sink into the trail and disappear. The process repeated many times until finally the rocks remained above the mud.

Crushing rocks for use as turnpike fill.

After quarrying came crushing which involved finding large rocks and using sledgehammers to reduce them to softball size rocks. The results were smaller size pieces that were stacked on top of the large sunken boulders.

Landscaping was the final stage of the turnpike where we used golf ball sized rocks and fill dirt to complete a smooth trail so hikers could travel on the trail without being sucked into the muck. Constructing that fifty-foot section of turnpike took the entire crew working for a full day.

We would return to our campsite at the end of the day. Each crewmember chose a night to become the cook and dishwasher. Meal times were enjoyable as we shared amusing stores of our past trail adventures. Evenings were spent around the campfire with jokes being told and songs being played.

As the sun began to set, everyone departed to their tents and the wolves began to howl. From the far ends of the lake, the howling would go back and forth for hours. Carnivores talking to each other just as we were doing around the campfire.

After seven days of work, we changed a muddy trail into an easily traversable pathway that future hikers will appreciate for decades into the future.

Trail Tales

The finished turnpike at Rainbow Lake.

The people you meet and the talents they have are every bit as enjoyable as the wild places you will visit.

Lost And Found

It was a warm Montana summer evening when we met at the trailhead to camp out – our trip would not officially begin until the next day. The crew leader, Megan, explained the work that we will be doing along the Continental Divide Trail (CDT).

The crew consisted of an experienced group of volunteers, primarily from the Helena and Kalispell areas of Montana. Among them was Dave, a short lean retiree. He casually introduced himself to me and mentioned that he loved to hike and run long distance trail races across the state. I asked him how you know where to run and what trails to take. He replied, "Oh, that's easy. You just follow the flagging."

The next morning we departed the trailhead for a long hike along the access trail into the CDT. This sixteen-mile stretch was along a wilderness stream and across a steep mountain pass that intersected multiple trail crossings, eventually joining the CDT.

Trail signs along the CDT.

The plan was to try to hike together, so no one would get lost, all the while stopping for rest breaks and lunch. If a crewmember came upon a trail junction, we were to stop and wait for the rest of the crew to catch up before proceeding.

Before tackling the pass, we stopped for lunch at a stream crossing where free-range cattle watched us from afar as we ate.

Trail Tales

Montana cattle ranchers transport their cattle to public lands for the summer grazing. These cattle roam the national forests until September when the ranchers round them up and truck them back to their ranches for the winter months. To an outsider they look like they are lost, but the ranchers know exactly where to find them.

Free-range cattle roaming along the trail.

Megan explained that next few miles will be a steep climb and since we hiked at different speeds, that we should meet at the top of the pass and wait until everyone arrives.

After a challenging climb, we summited the access trail that we had been following and stopped at the peak for a rest break before descending down to the CDT. At this point, we were tired and anxious to get to the campsite.

"Follow this trail down the mountain. It will join the CDT." acknowledged Megan. "Stay on the CDT, follow the blazes and we'll meet up at the campsite", she remarked.

We made a quick stop to refill our water bottles at a stream crossing where the side trail we had been following joined the CDT. The CDT is marked with white blazes and small signs. A single blaze means straight ahead. A double blaze means turn ahead -all standard formats for blazing hiking trails.

After a mile, the CDT turned right and side trail proceeded straight. Since it was getting close to dusk, we did not stop at the junction as we had been doing in the past to regroup but just powered along to get to the campsite.

Another mile passed and we reached the campsite, which was in a grove of trees next to a pasture on the CDT. We dropped our packs to begin to scout out kitchen and tent sites.

Megan, who was last in line, arrived at the campsite and did a head count. "Who are we missing? There are only seven of us!" she asked.

Robert, Dave's friend from Helena, said, "Dave's not here. He not must have made the turn and gone straight on that side trail".

A well-marked CDT trail in the Bob Marshall Wilderness Area.

Admittedly, some trail signs were confusing with arrows pointing in random directions. Hikers, to help those who followed behind them had modified some.

"That trail goes for four miles to the ranger cabin. I hope he realizes he missed the turn and comes back," Megan nervously explained. Dave failed to follow the blazes…he was lost.

Some trail signs can be confusing. Hikers to help those who follow behind them modify some.

With the sun slowly setting, Robert volunteered to go find his friend. Hopefully he would find Dave and be back by dark. After 16 miles of hiking, we were tired and none of us wanted to join in the search and rescue party, but everyone politely asked if he wanted company. Robert said, "No worries, I'll find him. Save some dinner for us," and off he went.

The rest of the crew set up their tents and we began making dinner. We were all very concerned about Dave and questioned how he successfully completes trail runs and marathons without getting lost.

Trail Tales

Three hours later, the light from two headlamps appeared in the dark from down the trail. Robert and Dave returned. Dave hiked all the way to the cabin and then stopped when he did not find the rest of the crew. Robert caught up with him and they retraced their steps for a total of eight miles.

The lost had been found!

It is not as much as where you are going but how you will get there.

Packers

Frank is a packer who volunteers in the Bob Marshall Wilderness area of Montana. He is a Ferrier by profession, but his passion is traveling through Montana's wilderness areas helping trail crews transport their tools and equipment from trailheads to work sites. He does so with the help of four legged friends.

Most trail crews that maintain trails in the eastern United States go out on trips that are three to five days in length. Crewmembers are expected to carry in their own camping gear, food and tools. Such was the case when working on the AT in Maine.

Western trail crews access more remote sections of trails and these trip lengths usually last five to seven days. The need to carry camping gear, tools and seven days of food adds to the weight of a person's pack. That level of difficulty requires the assistance of a packer like Frank.

Trail Tales

Packers are typically volunteers who own horses or mules, commonly referred to as stock, that agree to help the trail crews by using their horses or mules to carry the equipment to a remote job site. Russ and his son Var are packers based out of Kalispell, Montana. Russ owns an electrical contracting business in Kalispell but uses his time off to support trail crews working with a team of six horses in the Montana wilderness.

Frank traveling in the Bob Marshall Wilderness Area.

Frank is a mule lover and only travels with mules. Mules are the offspring of a female horse and a male donkey. A hybrid of a horse and a donkey. When a mule is bred from a large draft horse female and a mammoth jacks donkey the result is a massive animal weighing over 1200 lbs.

Mules have special traits that make them suitable as pack animals. Their eyes are set wider on their heads than horses letting them have a wider field of vision. This is especially helpful when navigating narrow trails. A mule's back is flatter than the backs of horses – much better for packing loads. They are less susceptible to illness, which means they can live long productive lives, commonly over 20 years.

Donkeys are characterized as fighters in dire situations. If a donkey becomes tangled up in a rope or leather lead, they will try to fight their way out. In a similar situation, a horse may panic to the point he hurts himself. However, a mule, in that same situation of being tangled up, will wait patiently for help. This is a big advantage when in the mountains with long strings of mules tied together.

Mules are also more intelligent than horses. If a mule says "no" it is for a reason, thus the phrase "Stubborn as a mule". A packer can tell a horse what to do but he must ask a mule.

When Frank decides to purchase a mule to use as a pack animal, he does not care about how the mule looks. Good-looking necks, ears, feet do not count. What he is most concerned about is its size and temperament. Big, strong, curious, approachable and good around people are qualities Frank considers most important.

Trail Tales

Frank invests much more than his time and stock to support a crew. Typically, he will meet the trail crew at a trailhead the evening before a trip. Frank has a pickup truck capable of pulling a large stock trailer carrying six to eight mules. The trailer will include the mules, saddles, bridles, food, along with tarps and ropes to secure the equipment to the stock. The investment Frank has made in his stock and gear is astounding, not to mention his expenses for traveling many miles to reach the trailhead.

Mule shenanigans in a backcountry corral.

As a packer, Frank is never seen alone. Along with the stock, that he was either riding or leading is another four-legged animal,

Trail Tales 21

a dog. A dog is a packer's best friend. His dog will travel with him along the trail. Never getting too far ahead or behind.

A packer's best friend.

One of the most valuable tools Franks carries is a scale. It is a hanging type scale with a loop on one end and a hook on the other. Before loading the stock, each box of equipment is carefully hung from the scale and weighed.

Based on the size of the stock being used the loads need to be between 50 to 75 pounds. Larger mules can carry 150 pounds, two 75-pound boxes on each side. Smaller or older mules can carry 100 pounds total. Equipment is added to or removed until the weight of the two boxes are equal and the load was balanced for the animal.

Equipment boxes loaded on a mule.

    Frank will wrap the equipment boxes with tarps, called manties, and then tie them with a rope to ensure nothing will come loose and fall out. Two equally weighted boxes are then hoisted onto each mule's saddle and attached with ropes.
    Once loaded, Frank will lead two or three mules strung together by their halters out on the trail at three miles per hour. The crewmembers, whose equipment Frank is transporting, will follow closely behind the stock to the worksite.

Trail Tales

In bear country, if the most valuable tool Frank is carrying is a scale, then the second most valuable tool is a revolver. A packer, with a gun prominently displayed on his hip, is a common sight on the trail. Protection on the hip!

Frank and other packers are valuable assets to those working in the remote wilderness. Their dedication of time and resources are extraordinary.

A pack string on the CDT.

Friends can make carrying heavy loads enjoyable.

Bridging The Gap

   While I spent many days maintaining hiking trails by cutting trees and clearing the trail corridor, I never was involved in building any structures in the wilderness. To lean some new skills I decided to join a Montana Wilderness Association (MWA) trail crew that was tasked with building a puncheon
   Our crew of eight was responsible for bridging the gap by installing a puncheon along a remote section of the Continental Divide Trail (CDT) in Montana. The US Forest Service deemed this a necessity to preserve the trail and allow hikers and horseback riders to pass this muddy section of trail.
   When even a turnpike is an impractical solution to drain water off the trail due to a stream crossing, bog or rocky tread; puncheons are the answer.

Trail Tales

A puncheon resembles a short bridge. It consists of decking made from sawed, treated timber attached to stringers that elevate the trail across the wet area. The stringers are 50 feet long and 8 to 10 inch diameter trees that were cut from trees near the jobsite. Side rails, called curbs, were then placed on the top of the decking to complete the structure.

Several months before our trip, the US Forest Service's pack mules transported the decking, nails and some and cached them near the worksite.

The puncheon had to be built across a 50-foot long muddy section of the trail where a small stream crossed the trail. When we arrived at the site, it was evident something needed to be done. Horses and mules traveling on this section sank into the muck. Hikers on the other hand, avoided the section by creating undesirable bypass trails. This only served to damage the surrounding flora.

We surveyed the site and developed a list of tasks that needed to be accomplished. The first job was to find two trees to act as sills for the stringers to sit on. They needed to be six feet long and 24 inches in diameter to support the weight.

Trail Tales

Sills act as a foundation for the puncheon.

We divided into two teams. One crew found two trees, cut them and debarked them. The others dug out the mud and muck from each end of the trail where the sills were to be laid. A seemly simple task that took an entire day.

The following day was a bigger challenge. We searched the woods for two equally sized 50-foot tall trees that were cut for stringers. The goal was to find these trees as close to the jobsite as possible so as avoid a long and heavy carry.

Out came the crosscut saw for felling and draw knives for debarking these monsters. It took a lot of brute strength to carry, roll, coerce and pry those two logs into place.

Stringers sitting on the sills.

    Day three on the site required some leveling activities to get the puncheon as level as possible. Gingerly trying not to be sucked into the mud, we straddled the sills and stringers so we could shave a little wood off here and there to get a near perfect fit.

    Some of the crew jumped into the mud, bravely accepting wet and soggy boots. Others tried a more creative method of keeping their feet dry by using plastic bags on their feet inside their boots. Despite our creative and heroic efforts, all of us returned to the campsite with extremely wet and muddy clothing. The campfire that night was one big circle of drying boots and socks.

Trail Tales 29

With the project's end in sight, we returned to the mud hole and began nailing the tread planks, which the Forest Service hauled in for us earlier in the season, to the stringers.

Tread boards for the deck of the puncheon.

These tread boards, which were one foot wide, four feet long and six inches thick, were durable enough to last for years and supported the weight of a horse or mule as they crossed over. With the tread boards in place and the curb rail installed, we posed for pictures of the completed project.

Trail Tales

Finished project.

Finishing a project like this puncheon is very satisfying. Each member learned from the other. We each brought skills to the project that were complimentary.

The ultimate satisfaction was witnessing three CDT thru hikers ceremoniously walk across the puncheon. Onward to Canada with dry feet ---Thanks to our team that bridged the gap!

One less tree to climb over, one less muddy patch to go around, makes for a pleasurable journey.

¡Hola! ¿Como Estás?

I found myself arriving late one May night on a flight from Atlanta into Lima, Peru. I desperately scanned the baggage claim area for other travelers who may be wearing a brown REI travel T-shirt. This was the shirt that I was given to wear as a key indicator to the other five crewmembers that I would be joining on my Recreational Equipment Inc. (REI) Lodge to Lodge Trek to Machu Picchu.

As we collected our bags from the baggage carousel, the group started to find each other. Nadja from Washington, Heather from California, Randy from Montana, Dianne from Colorado, Yi from California and myself from Georgia.

The six of us came from all parts of the United States to see Machu Picchu in a unique manner. We were going to hike the famous Inca Trail, not by camping out or sleeping under the stars, but by spending our nights in five-star mountain lodges.

Trail Tales   32

Each lodge was located along the Inca Trail, a one days hiking distance apart. Native contractors built the lodges two years earlier by using mules to haul all the equipment and supplies into the jobsite. The lodges were powered by powerful propane generators that provided electricity from 6:00am to 10:00pm. Satellite internet enabled guests to access email and websites. The staff included a native cook, house cleaner, bartender and masseuse.

Wayra Lodge along the Inca Trail in Peru.

Five mules and handlers carried our clothing, food and equipment from lodge to lodge. Our REI guides, Raul, and his

Trail Tales

assistant, Claudio, were bilingual natives of Peru who guided us along the trail.

Our duffle bags of clothing and gear were strapped to a mule after breakfast each morning and upon arrival were placed in our room at the next lodge. Each crewmember only had to carry a daypack, which made the trek extremely enjoyable!

After hiking in from the trailhead, we arrived at our first lodge at 2:00pm. Raul introduced us to the lodge staff, gave us keys to our room and requested that we return to the lobby for dinner at 7:00pm

Some of the crewmembers were fighting jet lag and took naps. Others read or made use of the internet that afternoon.

With five hours until dinner, I needed something to do. I noticed the lodge had a large fireplace with a dwindling wood supply. I asked Raul where they store their firewood and he said "down the trail by the barn."

I headed off to the barn and next to it I found an axe and a pile of wood. Taking off my jacket, I began to chop wood. A short time later Raul walked down to check on the crazy American.

"What are you doing?" asked Raul. "Chopping some wood for the fireplace," I replied.

"But Bob, guests don't need to work while they are on vacation," Raul replied. I smiled, gave him a thumbs up and went back to the chopping block.

After a few hours of chopping wood, it was getting close to dinnertime and I had worked up an appetite. One of the mule handlers walked by.

"¡Hola! ¿Como estás?" was my greeting. He waved, replied back in Spanish. I didn't understand a word he said, but I smiled. After taking three years of high school Spanish and not applying it for another 40 years, my vocabulary was limited. ¡Hola! ¿Como estás? was the limit.

The Lodge's firewood pile and chopping block.

The next day, we rose with the sun and enjoyed a fantastic Peruvian breakfast comprised of eggs to order, fresh fruit and home baked pastries. We were on the trail to the next lodge by 8:00am. Raul guided us along the trail, stopping occasionally for

Trail Tales 35

rest breaks at scenic points of interest. Raul's knowledge of the history, people and culture of Peru was astounding.

We stopped for lunch at a mountain pass and arrived at the next lodge by midafternoon. After a traditional Peruvian dinner of chicken, rice, beans, fresh baked bread and desserts; some crewmembers read while others surfed the internet. I, however, needed something to do to pass the time before lights out.

I found a deck of cards and asked if anyone wanted to play cards. Claudio was the only one who expressed an interest.

"What should we play?" he asked. "Claudio, teach me to play poker," I replied.

"Aw, Bob. We need more than just the two of us and we need some chips."

There, on our table, was a vase of dried flowers with decorative red beans in the bottom of the vase keeping them upright. I dipped my hand in the vase and out came red beans that would become our poker chips. However, we still needed more players.

The every-ready to serve lodge staff were sitting close by ... looking quite bored now since everyone did not need their service.

"What about them?" I said to Claudio and pointing their way. "They are working," he said.

"They don't look like they are working to me. How about asking them if they want to join in and have some fun?" A conversation took place in Spanish. I, of course, had no clue as to what they was said, but soon there were four more poker players at the table.

Learning to play poker in Peru.

The game began as Claudio taught all of us how to play poker, in Spanish for the staff and in English for me. The lodge crew was having a great time and I sensed this might be the first time they were ever invited to play a game with the guests.

We played until almost 10pm when we needed to stop before the power went out for the night. I lost most of my red beans while the lodge crew and Claudio did quite well.

Lesson learned. Playing poker with a Spanish-speaking group of players can make you lose many beans. On the bright side, you can make new friends.

The next morning, after enjoying a hearty breakfast, we departed for the trek to the next lodge. All of my poker-playing friends waved goodbye.

As we began to walk down the trail away from the lodge, the cook yelled out "Adios, No carrera como jugador de poke".

I asked Claudio to interpret for me. He laughed and said, "Do not consider a career as a poker player," and off we went down the trail.

My poker-playing friends in Peru.

Language barriers can make a trail adventure memorable.

Glacier Bound

Alaska. I always consider it a special state to visit, especially after traveling there on a summer vacation with my family. I thought climbing Mount Denali (formerly Mount McKinley) would be the ultimate Alaska adventure. Unfortunately, my limited vacation allotment at work made that an impossibility. My wife also had concerns about my being gone for four weeks --- the time it would take to climb the mountain. We eventually settled on a compromise. I enrolled in a six-day climbing course scheduled for the Eldridge Glacier in July.

I flew into Anchorage and drove to the location of the course in Talkeetna where I met the other participants in the course. Earl was a high school orchestra teacher. Ken was an electrician on the Alaska pipeline. Matt and John were bankers from Houston. Addy, was a recent college graduate.

Our instructors for the course Josh, Adam and Travis were experienced mountain guides. Travis proved to be an excellent

Trail Tales 40

cook. After they briefed us on the schedule for the day, we packed our food, double checked our gear and secured our permits from the National Park Service for the trip into the Denali National Park.

We boarded a 1956 DeHavilland Beaver prop plane for the short flight to the glacier. The Beaver is a plane of choice in Alaska -- the pilot can raise and lower skis for soft snow landings, making it perfect for carrying climbers into the backcountry and landing on glaciers.

Glacier landing strip on the Eldridge Glacier in Alaska.

After circling the glacier to assess the landing area and wind conditions, the pilot landed uphill on the glacier. We quickly unloaded our gear. As the pilot was getting ready to take off for Talkeetna, he called to us, "See you in six days!"

For the next four days, we learned about snow camping and climbing skills, including: the proper way to pitch a tent in the snow; how to set up a snow kitchen; what are the best snowshoeing techniques; how to climb icy peaks safely; and how to perform a crevasse rescue in case a crewmember disappeared into a vast chasm.

By the fourth evening, the winds increased and snow began to fall. Snowing in July--only in Alaska.

The snow continued for two days as we hibernated in our small two-person tents. Reading was our only activity. When we needed a break, we went outside to remove the snow buildup on the tent so it would not collapse.

On day number six, we used a satellite phone to call the air taxi service to find out when our pickup would arrive. "Not today," was the response. The snow falling on the glacier meant there were low clouds. It also meant it was raining in Talkeetna, which would limit the pilot's visibility to fly.

Travis - Climbing Instructor, Guide, and Head Cook.

Day seven the snow stopped and the work began. With our snowshoes, we stomped out to the runway. Walking up and down the runway, over, and over again, we packed the new snow down. This would help the pilot distinguish the runway from the unpacked snowfields.

Later that afternoon we called again to get a pickup time confirmed. The pilot was not confident he would be able to land safely and pick us up. Conservation mode began.

We were running low on many vital supplies. We had planned for a six-day trip. It now was approaching eight days. Fuel for our camping stoves was running low. We used the stoves for cooking, but more importantly, we used them to melt snow into drinkable water.

Campsite on the Eldridge Glacier Alaska, overlooking the landing strip.

We began to ration food supplies by cutting back on our portions. We were critically low on toilet paper and had to use chapters of our paperbacks that we have already read as a substitute. Our fun six-day trek in Alaska was turning into a trek that tested our patience.

By day eight, it became a mental game. We tried to stay positive and pass the time best as we could. Some crewmembers read and listened to music. Others schemed about the possibility of hiking out – a nice dream, but it was not going to happen.

I needed a more active outlet and strapped on snowshoes to make another lap stamping out the runway.

A long day eight ended and day nine began with our food supplies at critical levels. After a breakfast of white rice with some dry milk added to make it tolerable, we placed another call to the pilot.

"I think I may be able to come to get you today," was the response. "I'll fly over and take a look."

One hour later we heard a plane approaching. The pilot circled the glacier and made his approach landing uphill on our firmly packed runway. We were excited that very soon we would be off the glacier. Then we noticed he was flying a Cessna 182 and only had space for three of us.

We drew straws and three of our team members climbed into the plane. The pilot acknowledged that he now knows he can safely land on the glacier and he will send a larger plane to get the rest of us.

Trail Tales

Alaska Air Taxi: 1956 DeHavilland Beaver.

Two hours later a DeHavilland Beaver is back making an approach to land. It landed uphill and turned a hard right to be ready for a downhill takeoff. The plane stopped and the pilot jumped out followed by four tourists who came along for a flightseeing tour of Denali. The visitors were excited to experience the thrill of a glacier landing.

The tourists are amazed we are on the glacier, and we were amazed at how kind they were to us. How kind? Well, for the hour flight back to Talkeetna, they tolerated us --six hungry, scraggly, smelly glacier bound climbers looking for a ride home.

Patience, tolerance, and fortitude can turn a bad experience into a delight.

On A Mission

Hikers fall into three different categories. Casual hikers are those out for a day hike and usually never stray far from the trailhead. Backpackers are individuals who want to hike farther than casual hikers, typically carrying all their food and supplies with them while hiking for multiple days. Thru-hikers are hikers who are determined to hike an entire trail such as the AT, CDT or PCT in one trip. These individuals are on a mission!

Thru-hikers come from the far reaches of the United States and the world to hike these trails. Some are recent high school or college graduates looking to experience the trail before starting a career. Others are recently retired and are anxious to fulfill a lifelong dream. Their mission is to finish the trail and to celebrate at the monument marking the end of the trail.

A thru-hike of the AT, which is 2,190 miles long, will take an average hiker between five and seven months to complete. This means hiking an average of 15 to 20 miles per day. Thru-hikers usually take a weekly rest day to restock their food supplies, shower and do some wash. Currently, the fastest AT thru hiker record stands at 41 days, seven hours and 39 minutes, an average of 63 miles per day.

While maintaining trails on the AT, CDT and PCT, I was able to meet many thru-hikers. As each thru hiker passed the work crew, he or she would remark, "Thank you for all you do!" Thru-hikers really appreciate the work volunteers do such as cutting out blowdowns, cleaning out water bars and keeping the trail in good condition.

Hikers at the terminus of the AT on Mt Katahdin Maine.

Each thru-hiker has a trail name, he uses that name when meeting others and signing log books. Some individuals choose a name before starting the hike. Most wait to be dubbed with that name by other hikers.

Trail Tales

A trail name may be based on where you are from. I met a hiker from Iowa who went by the name Soybean. Other names are based on a physical appearance such as Stringbean, who was a tall, lankly hiker. That trail name remains with the hiker forever.

Hikers enjoying the rainy weather.

One Sunday afternoon while working on the AT in Maine, two young women quickly passed us. They had recently graduated from college starting the hike on April 4th in Georgia and used the trail names Snickers and Granola. They expected to finish on Mount Katahdin on August 20th. We were working on a section that was 50 miles from the AT terminus and these women were on a mission to finish in three days.

Most hikers who passed us would quickly say hello and we would wish them good luck. Some asked about the weather forecast for the next few days. Others would drop their packs, take a break and we would have a wonderful conversation.

Such was the case on the CDT while working on building the puncheons through the muck. Three 20-year-old hikers came down the trail and stopped for a break. They were from different states and started the CDT days apart but were hiking together.

This trio was on a mission to finish the CDT at the Canadian border in ten days. They were hoping to get there before the first snowfall but had plenty of time to stop and talk with our crew. We ceremoniously let each of them drive a spike into the puncheon's decking and made them honorary CDT trail maintainers.

All thru-hikers commit significant time and money to hike these trails. Some more so than others. Thermometer was a CDT thru-hiker who passed me on the trail when I was working in Montana. He was Korean, had started at the Mexican border, and was heading north to Canada. Originally, he planned to hike the PCT but when he arrived in California and learned about the deep snow in the Sierras that was preventing hikers from traveling along the PCT, he changed plans.

He took a train to New Mexico and started north on the CDT. He had a small thermometer on his pack and when I asked for his "trail name", he pointed to it. The language barrier did not stop him from letting me know his trail name was Thermometer. On that cold and rainy day, he was by himself without any other hikers for miles around, but he was on a mission to finish.

Stopping to view the surroundings will create memories to last.

Simply Dynamite

Trail hazards come in many forms. Hikers frequently have to deal with downed trees, stream crossings, mud hole diversions and wild animals.

Stream crossings will slow a hiker down, but an experienced one will jump across some rocks in the stream without even getting a toe wet. Mud holes take more finesse and may require some careful foot placements at the edge of the trail to avoid a boot full of mud. Wild animals though require many skills.

Wild animals on the trail come in all sizes, from three-inch tall chipmunks to eight-foot tall moose and everything in between. Most animals are more afraid of humans then humans are afraid of them, but precautions are always justified. Such was the case while hiking in the Bob Marshall Wilderness.

The "Bob", as locals call it, is a wilderness area in northwest Montana, which is named after Bob Marshall (1901-1939). Bob was an early forester, conservationist and co-founder of the Wilderness Society. This wilderness area, designated in 1964, extends for 60 miles along the Continental Divide and encompasses over one million acres.

Since it is designated a wilderness area, no mechanical equipment, such as cars, trucks, ATV's, etc. are permitted on the over 1,800 miles of trails. The trails are open to foot and stock use only.

The Chinese Wall in the Bob Marshall Wilderness Area.

I signed up to join a trail crew that was heading north along the Continental Divide Trail (CDT) to an area called the Chinese Wall. The Chinese Wall is a large cliff that extends for 40 miles along the CDT. This trail crew's project involved cleaning out water bars along the trail to reduce erosion. During the summer months,

Trail Tales

traffic in this area are thru-hikers, weekend backpackers and pack teams of backcountry equestrians.

The pack teams are well equipped. Commonly a lead rider or wrangler who knows the area and the trails extremely well will lead the group. This lead rider will be guiding a string of two or three other horses or mules loaded with food and camping equipment for the group. Behind them will be the riders who will enjoy riding, fishing, hiking and relaxing around the campfire for the next five to seven days. Most trips go as planned but sometimes problems occur and action is needed.

A Pack team in the Bob Marshall Wilderness Area.

Trail Tales 54

My trail crew began our trek early in the morning of August 8th. Ten miles in on the trail there was an orange sign nailed to a tree. It read, "Warning - Be Alert -500 feet, August 5th."

When horses or mules break a leg or have a serious medical problem and cannot proceed, the wrangler needs to take action.

Carcass warning sign in the Bob Marshall Wilderness.

Trail Tales

Because the Bob Marshall is a wilderness area, no trucks or trailers can access the remote trail and provide assistance. Thus, the common action to take when a horse or mule breaks a leg and is in pain is to put it down.

However, a carcass of a dead horse or mule on a heavily traveled trail like the CDT is hazard. Over time, the carcass will rot and return to the earth, but that could be months. The smell of a rotting carcass is not a pleasant experience for the passing hikers and riders.

Even more of a concern is the carcass will attract other wild animals, such as grizzly bears, who will feed on the meat and potentially defend its bounty by attacking others who pass nearby. Thus, the packers need to do something with the carcass quickly.

Packers, along with their food, camping gear and equipment, carry VHF radios. These radios have the capability for communication with US Forest Service personnel in nearby lookout towers and regional offices. The packer can relay the location of the incident and request assistance.

The US Forest Service annually hires over 3,000 seasonal employees who work building trails, enhancing wildlife habitat and improving historic landmarks. Some of these employees are specially trained to handle crises such as a carcass on the trail. When they hear a request for help, a team of forest service employees ride into the carcass site. This journey may take two or three days.

Once onsite, they assess the situation. If the carcass can be easily buried, they bury it. In most cases that is not easily done. Dynamite is the answer.

Trail Tales

By strategically placing 100 pounds of TNT, with a push of the plunger, the carcass is transformed into a shower of tiny pieces scattered across the area. The hazard is eliminated – no longer an attraction to grizzly bears. The trail is safe to pass. Simply dynamite!

We were fortunate enough during this CDT maintenance project not to experience any grizzly bears. Our travels through the Bob Marshall Wilderness were safer thanks to the US Forest Service and their creative methods for dealing with hazards.

Problems sometimes require creative solutions.

Cut It Out

Trees across trails are the most common trail hazard that impedes the progress of a hiker. Some trees can be easily stepped over. Others block the trail to the point that a hiker will have to climb over or go around the obstacle. These trees require a trail maintenance crew to cut them out.

On most national forests, crews with chainsaws can make quick work of a tree across the trail. With two or three cuts, a tree can be cut out and removed from the pathway. In designated wilderness areas, no chainsaws are allowed. The tool of choice is a crosscut saw.

I was fortunate to be able to join a Washington Trail Association (WTA) Backcountry Response crew one summer. My son Kyle joined me. Our job for five days was to remove trees along Trail 970 near Bumping Lake, Washington. Our crew of 10 volunteers was comprised of eight men and two women. An experienced crosscut sawyer named Gary was our fearless leader.

Trail Tales 58

Gary retired from the Boeing Corporation as a computer programmer. He now volunteers to lead maintenance trips in Washington's Cascade Mountains. Paul, a retired CPA, and David, who worked for many years in transportation and logistics, were the assistant crew leaders.

Crew leader Gary surrounded by other crew members.

The trailhead where we met was a campsite at the end of the Bumping River Road, a 30 mile gravel forest service access road. Driving carefully along the road in my rental car, I passed campsites and crossed a number of streams on wooden bridges, all constructed by US Forest Service personnel.

Trail Tales 59

The views along the road were spectacular. About 24 miles into the journey, I approached a road intersection and parked at the junction where three large white pickup trucks. Eighteen individual in green and yellow garb were standing outside the trucks. Looking tired and worn out, they are a US Forest Service Hotshot crew that just finished extinguishing a lighting strike forest fire a short distance from the trailhead. These young and energetic individuals were experienced wildland forest fighters whose responsibility it was to be first on the scene of a fire and to quickly control and extinguish it.

At the trailhead, I met the other members of the crew, who had a wide variety of experience in trail maintenance. For some, using a crosscut saw was a new experience. For others, it is their passion. We agreed to get an early start the next morning since there were miles of trail to hike and many trees to be removed.

We woke at sunrise and packed our tents, food and equipment in our backpacks. We departed the campsite by 8:00am. Gary, Paul and David gave us a safety talk and reminded everyone of the need to be very careful while working. If an injury should occur, help would be hours away and access would be challenging for EMTs and rescue personnel. We shouldered our packs, grabbed our tools and set off to the first tree.

Being on a crosscut crew was like being part of a big outdoor hide and seek game. Hikers report to the WTA that there are trees across the trail, but the exact location and number of them always remained a mystery.

A crew can hike for miles and not find a tree. Once a tree is found, the next one can be 10 feet away. This trip was no exception. Trees were reported along Trail 970, but none of us was sure of the number, sizes or locations. Therefore, the game began.

Removing a large Pine tree with a crosscut saw on the trail.

Trail Tales

We hiked for an hour before we met the first obstacle. A large 30-inch diameter White Pine tree was across the trail. Hikers had to climb over this monster to get around it. This tree would require teamwork.

With small handsaws, crewmembers carefully removed the branches from the tree and got them out of the way and off the trail. We assessed the tree's angle and direction to make sure we would be in a safe position and not be crushed by a rolling pine tree when we finished cutting

Gary prepared the five-foot crosscut saw for action. He taught us how to hold the saw safely while the handles were attached. He removed the scabbard that protects the teeth of the saw to show us the cutting and raking teeth. Gary is not only an excellent sawyer but he sharpens all of his saws by hand making sure they are extremely sharp and ready for cutting.

Kyle, an experienced hiker but crosscut novice said, "What's next Gary?" Crew leader Gary replied, "Let's cut it out," and the work began.

While two crewmembers positioned themselves up and down the trail as lookouts for hikers who may arrive while we are cutting, two others began to saw. Gary, with the patience of a saint, directed the action and coached them on their technique. After a few minutes of cutting, two others relieved the first two and the sawing continued.

As we neared the end of the first cut, wedges had to be inserted into the top of the cut to keep the saw from sticking and binding. One crewmember pounded the red plastic wedges into the kerf and the sawing continued.

This was a "two cut" tree meaning it would take two cuts to remove a segment of the tree from the trail. Some trees can be removed in one cut while others may take three or four. The less cuts the better - more efficient and less labor.

Single bucking a tree with a crosscut saw requires skill.

The first cut was completed and the crew started on the second. More wedges were added to the second cut to prevent the saw from binding. As the sawyers were finishing the second cut, progress slowed.

The crew moved to a safe spot in case the tree rolled after the sawyers finished the second cut. With a thud, a four-foot long chunk of tree dropped to the ground on the trail.

The challenge now became to remove the pine segment out of the trail. While being coached by Gary, four crewmembers sat on the ground, feet on the tree, knees bent. On the count of three, with their legs, they pushed the tree off the trail into the woods. Congratulatory high fivees ensued. Hikers once again were free to pass. Tools were collected and the crew hiked to the next obstacle.

For the next four days, the crew removed both small and large trees along Trail 970. Some took minutes to remove while others took hours. A typical day was working from 7:00am to 4:00pm, hiking 2.5 miles and cutting out 22 trees. We spent our nights at campsites close to the trail and would be asleep by 8:00pm

While hiking out on our last day, it was getting late and we approached a large Western White Pine that was four-foot in diameter. This tree was the largest we had seen on the trip and it would take some time to remove it.

Concerned about time, Gary asked the crew, "What do you want to do? It's getting late. We can leave it for another crew if you want."

Trail Tales

After four days of crosscutting trees, we now considered ourselves experienced sawyers. We looked at each other and thought, no way are we leaving this job for the next crew.

We replied in unison, "Let's cut it out," and the work began!

Team efforts make a large task easy.

Come Back At 4:00pm

   The Grand Canyon is one of the United States' most visited national parks. Over four million people visit the canyon each year. The summer months are the most popular times to visit the park, and hordes of tourists come to view the natural wonder. Most visitors will ride busses along the rim. Few will venture below the rim, and those few included me.

   Camping reservations at the park required advance planning. A backcountry camping permit can be requested from the park up to four months in advance. I planned to visit the park in June so in April I sent in my request and received permission to camp for one night at the Bright Angel Campground, which is at the base of the Grand Canyon.

   After spending the night in a Flagstaff motel, we departed early for the park, arriving at the park entrance shortly after 8:00am. I followed the park map to the Backcountry Information Center to check in for the hike and begin the trek down the canyon.

Trail Tales

The Bright Angel Trail, which begins at the southern rim of the Grand Canyon, is a popular trail to reach the bottom of the canyon. From an elevation of 6,840 feet, a hiker will descend to 4,350 feet, which requires a 9.5-mile hike.

Bright Angel Trail sign at the South Rim.

The trail which passes multiple resting points called "Resthouses," skirts the Indian Garden Campground, crosses the Colorado River and ends at the Bright Angel Campground

Temperatures can become extreme during a July afternoon in the park. Hikers are encouraged to depart early before hiking to the bottom as well as when hiking from the bottom up to the rims. By arriving early in the morning, I planned to avoid the hot afternoon sun.

Trail Tales

The park service ranger greeted me with a smile. "I'm here to check in for my hike down to the Bright Angel Campground," I said. "My son and I have reservations for tonight."

The ranger checked his computer screen and said, "Yes, party of two for tonight. I see you have a reservation, but you are way too late to hike to the bottom."

"Too late? It's only 9:00am and we should have plenty of time to hike down before it gets too hot." I replied.

"I understand. Is this your first visit the park?" the ranger asked. Yes, it was our first visit to the park. We were excited to see the canyon from an upclose perspective by hiking down and camping at the bottom - something few visitors even consider.

"Here is my suggestion," said the Ranger. "Visit some of the overlooks, take a few pictures, stop in some of the gift shops and enjoy a pleasant lunch with maybe a cold ice tea."

"That sounds great." I responded. "But our reservation that we made four months ago is only good for tonight."

The Ranger remarked, "You two look like you have backpacked before. Enjoy the canyon from the rim and come back here at 4:00pm".

We were puzzled. Why would he recommend we start the hike at 4:00pm in the afternoon? Trusting that he knew best, we enjoyed the vistas and South Rim's walking trails while impatiently waiting for 4:00pm to arrive.

We double-checked our food, water and camping gear we would need for the hike. Anything extra was left in the car. No need for non-essentials or luxury items on this trip. Hiking down would be hard. Coming up the next morning would be even harder!

Trail Tales 68

At 4:00pm, we returned to the Backcountry Information Center. The same ranger we met this morning was still assisting guests with trail suggestions and advice.

We checked in again and he confirmed the reservation. He then said, "Now is the time to go. Enjoy the hike". And off we went!

Preparing to depart down the Bright Angel Trail.

As we progressed down the trail, we passed a few hikers coming up. They looked very much unprepared. Hiking in sneakers, carrying a small bottle of water, without any sun protection, we wondered just how far they went down before deciding to return.

Trail Tales

As we hiked down and arrived at the Lower Tunnel, a distance of less than one mile, a large round thermometer was displaying a temperature of 116 degrees. The sun was behind some peaks and trail was starting to become shaded. As we continued down to the first Resthouse, the temperatures seemed to be getting cooler and the shade increased.

The Bright Angel Trail in the afternoon shade.

At 3-Mile Resthouse we stopped for a break. The thermometer read 97 degrees. It was getting cooler with each mile we hiked. The Ranger knew that we would be hiking in cooler temperatures if we waited for the hot afternoon sun to pass. "Come back at 4:00pm" was great advice.

As we approached the River Resthouse, the sun was setting. Hiking along the river reminded me of hiking along a beach with big sand dunes. Mounds of river sand made the trail a challenge. With each step we would take, our feet would sink into the sand - postholing in the sand. Never would have guessed we would be hiking across a beach at the bottom of the Grand Canyon.

At the end of the beach, there was a suspension bridge that crossed the Colorado River. Since the sun was long gone, we dug our headlamps out of our packs. We carefully crossed the suspension bridge to the north side of the river.

With less than two miles to go to the campground, we hiked slower and more cautiously than earlier. Not wanting to take a wrong turn in the dark, we followed the trail past a trail junction that led to the north rim and arrived at the campground at 9:00pm, about a five-hour hike rim to canyon.

Using our headlamps, we searched for a campsite. Most sites were occupied by those campers who chose to depart the south rim very early in the morning and arrived before the hot afternoon sun. We found an empty site, laid down a ground cloth on which we placed our sleeping bags, and cowboy camped for the night.

Camping under the stars without a tent as the cowboys used to do was an amazing night. The moon was full and the stars were shining brightly, with some shooting across the sky. Bats darted above our heads chasing insects.

It was hard to go to sleep with such an amazing free show going on above our heads. We discussed what time we needed to depart for the rim in the morning. Because the sun rose at 5:00am

Trail Tales

and we thought that would be a good time to depart, we set our alarms on our watches for 5:00am.

We got very little sleep that evening. At 4:00am, we were awake and decided to pack up and get out. Most other campers were still sleeping so as quietly as possible, we departed for the South Rim. We estimated that five hours down would mean a longer trip up and we wanted to be there before the mid-day heat wave started.

The Bright Angel Trail ascends from the bottom of the canyon to the South Rim.

Retracing our route, we hiked in the dark for about an hour and then continued to ascend the trail in the early morning light. After a quick stop at Indian Garden Campground for a snack and

Trail Tales

to refill our water bottles, we arrived at the canyon rim at 10:00am, a six-hour return trip with 2,500 feet of elevation gain over 9.5 miles. Very commendable.

We walked over to the Backcountry Information Center to check out and inform the Ranger that we were off the trail safely.

The same Ranger who gave us the excellent advice the day before about waiting out the hot sun was advising another group of hikers.

"Come back at 4:00pm," he remarked to the group. They looked very puzzled.

"Come back at 4:00pm. You won't be disappointed," we said in unison.

It is puzzling at times to see positive results from a potentially negative situation.

Trail Security

Security on a trail is a concern for every hiker. Concerns about secure trails include if the stream and river crossings are passable, if the shelters are safe from wild animals and if the people you meet along the trail are trustworthy individuals and not a threat to your life. Rarely have I ever been asked to be a security guard on a trail, except in Alaska.

We arrived at the Anchorage airport at 2am on a Saturday morning in March. My son Kyle and I flew all night to arrive at a surprisingly busy airport, given the early morning hours. We picked up a rental car and drove to our nearby hotel.

On the drive to the hotel Kyle commented, "Wouldn't it be great if we would see a moose on this trip?" Alaska has a surprisingly large population of moose and they can appear in the most unexpected places.

As we parked the car at the hotel and collected our luggage from the trunk, I turned to my left and was astonished by what I saw.

Trail Tales

I said, "Look to your left and what do you see?"

Just across the street from the hotel stood a Bull Moose, wandering around the edge of the snow and ice covered Lake Hoods – a sight more commonly seen in Alaska than most people would imagine. A moose was not the only animal we would see on this trip.

Kyle and I were in Anchorage for the start of the Iditarod Trail Sled Dog Race. The race is an annual event held on the second weekend in March. The course runs from Anchorage to Nome.

The 1925 serum run to Nome was known then as the "Great Race of Mercy." It occurred when a diphtheria epidemic threatened Nome. Nome residents needed the antitoxin, and the nearest location for resupply was Anchorage, almost 1,000 miles away. The only way to get the serum to Nome in the winter was sled dogs.

The race today is called "The Last Great Race." It began in 1973 with 34 mushers. Today, it follows parts of the historic trail. Over time, the field has grown to over 70 mushers.

For the race to be successful, it requires hundreds of volunteers. These individuals register participants, provide veterinary care to the dogs, man checkpoints along the trail and provide setup and security at the start of the race.

Security at any large event is always a concern for the organizers of the event. Police, military and most professional security individuals have extensive training in crowd control, emergency procedures, identifying dangerous situations and how to carry the appropriate equipment for emergencies.

When we volunteered for the Iditarod Security, we knew none of those professional security concepts. We decided on an

Trail Tales

informal Iditarod Race Security Motto: Smile-Be Nice-Everything will work out well!

Iditarod Trail Security Arm Band.

    The start of the Iditarod Race was on Saturday morning in Anchorage. It was a fun, ceremonial start and the mushers and dogs leisurely ran through the streets of Anchorage. Fans lined the course with high fives for the teams as they passed by.
    The following afternoon, the official start, was a less festive event. We were instructed to arrive at the community building in Willow, Alaska at 7:00am for our setup and security assignments. Willow is a two-hour drive north of Anchorage so we departed the

Trail Tales

hotel at 5:00am tired but with excitement. The race officially began on Willow Lake and headed north to Nome along the Iditarod trail.

Willow was established in 1897 when miners found gold in Willow Creek. In 1920, the Alaskan Railroad built a station in the town. Several years later, access to the town was made easier when the Alaska Parks Highway was built and passed though the town. Today, Willow Lake is surrounded by vacation cabins for seasonal use.

The starting line of the Last Great Race in Willow, AK.

Sunday was a beautiful sunny day. It was race day. The temperature was eight degrees with an expected high around 15.

Trail Tales

The lake was frozen solid and had two feet of snow on top of the crusty surface.

As a security volunteer, we joined six others who were local Alaskans and took orders from the volunteer security coordinator. Jack, our leader for the day, began to discuss the assignments.

The first task was to set up a security fence from the starting line at the community hall across the lake. The lake is one half mile wide so this fence was no small task.

Laying out the orange plastic fence from one side of the lake to the other required teamwork. We created a chute 20 feet wide between the two rows of fence. Every 100 yards, we left a break in the fence so the crowds could cross from one side to the other.

As members of the security team, we had to staff the breaks in the fence to make sure no one crossed when a musher and dog team were departing the starting line.

To hold the fence upright, every 10 feet a wooden stake four feet long was stuck through the fence and pounded into the snow. Just like the lake, the snow was frozen. Hammering stakes

Trail Tales

into frozen snow and ice was not easy task. It was slow going, but even with the chilly temperatures, we began to work up a sweat.

Iditarod Security Fence on Willow Lake, AK

After four hours of hard work, we finished the starting line chute and Jack assigned us to our security stations. We were assigned to staff a VIP area right at the starting gate. This was an excellent area to view the start of the race. Jack told us only individuals with VIP lanyards should be admitted to this area. This was a serious job assignment!

The mushers began to line up at the starting gate at 1:00pm and were dispatched down the chute every two minutes. Spectators would walk by and ask if they could enter the viewing area. Remembering our security motto: Smile- Be Nice- Everything will work out well, we did just that.

"Sorry this is for VIPs only, but there are great viewing places further down the chute," was my response.

By 4:00pm, all of the mushers departed Willow Lake for Nome. The fastest mushers traveled all day and night, resting and feeding the dogs along the trail. They would arrive in Nome in eight days. Other mushers set a more leisurely pace. Above all else, all participants wanted to finish safely with a team of healthy dogs.

On Sunday night, we returned to Anchorage and arrived at the airport. While passing through the airport security area, the officer asked, "What were you doing at the Iditarod?"

Remembering our Iditarod Security Motto: We smiled. We were nice. We replied "Trail Security". And off to the plane we went!

A warm smile can change an adversarial encounter into a positive outcome.

Trail Tales

Watch Your Step

On one summer climbing trip, five friends and I challenged ourselves to making the trek to the summit of Mount Rainier. This was the last leg of a three-day climb to our final destination. As the six of us stood on the snowy slope of the Emmons Glacier, Scott called out, "Watch your step!"

Mount Rainier is a large volcanic mountain located within Mount Rainier National Park. It sits 60 miles southeast of Seattle, Washington, and is a popular destinaton for climbers and mountaineers. With an elevation of 14,411 feet, Mount Rainier is the highest mountain in the continental United States. As beautiful as it is rugged, because of the large amounts of glacier ice, it is dangerous mountain to climb.

With 26 major glaciers and permanent snow fields, Mount Rainier is the most glacieated peak in the lower 48 states. The summit is topped by two volcanic craters. Geothermal heat keeps the rims of both craters free of ice and snow.

Climbing Mount Rainier is difficult and requires traversing large trecherous glaciers. The climb to the summit takes two to three days. The appoximate successful summit rate is 50% --weather being one of the key reasons for failure.

Each climber is required to posses some level of technical climbing skills. The climb requires the use of crampons, ice axes and ropes. Proficiency in crevase rescue skills is strongly encouraged.

Crevasses on the Emmons Glacier Mount Rainier.

There are two routes to reach the summit of Mount Rainier. Ninety percent of the climbers follow the Disappointment

Trail Tales

Cleaver Route which is on the southeast face via Camp Muir - named after John Muir who climbed the mountain in 1888.

The Emmons Glacier Route on the northeast face, is an alternative route passing through Camp Schurman, at 9,500 feet which is a glacial campsite.

Rock and ice falls, avalanches and hypothermia result in two deaths each year. Solo climbers risk their lives on such a unforginging mountain. Climbing as a group of six is considered a safe climbing team.

Our climb began on a Saturday morning at Mount Rainier National Park's White River Campground. After applying for a climbing permit, we checked our gear, food and supplies to be sure everything we needed for a safe trip was in our packs.

We climbed from 4,400 feet along a flowing river to the base of the Inner Glacier. We stopped here to change from our hiking boots to our climbing boots. We took the precaution of roping up.

Roping up -- attaching a climbing rope between three climbers, one on each end of the rope and one in the middle. In the event one individual steps into a deep crevasse, the other two climbers would be able to prevent the climber falling further and they could perform a rescue.

A crevasse is a deep, open crack in a glacier. Crevasses form as a result of the movement of the ice on the glacier, and crevasses can be as deep as 120 feet and hundreds of feet long.

A crevasse may be covered, but not filled, by a snow bridge from the previous years' of snow. Occasionally, some snow bridges will sag and provide a visual clue to the climber that a

Trail Tales

crevasse is present. Unfortunately, most crevasses are invisible to climbers and are potentially lethal to anyone crossing them - thereby causing the snow bridge to collapse.

It is imperative that climbers on Mount Rainier beaware of the changing weather patterns.

As we began ascending the Inner Glacier, a weather front moved in and the fog came with it. "Watch your step," each of us yelled as we slowly worked our way up the trail.

Climbing Mt. Rainier's Inner Glacier in the fog.

Trail Tales

A crack in the glacier indicates a potential crevasse.

Thankfully, we carefully climbed to a safe campsite at Camp Curtis on the glacier at 9,000 feet.

On day two, the weather changed again. The fog departed and the summer sun rose on the east side of the mountain. We departed the campsite and continued to ascend the Emmons Glacier to Camp Shuman at 9,500 feet.

There was a Ranger Station at Camp Shuman that was manned by experienced park service mountaineers who are available to assist with a rescue if needed.

Trail Tales

After pitching our tents, we reviewed safety procedures and practiced some crevasse rescues before making our final plans for our journey to the summit the next day.

Campsite at Camp Schuman on the Emmons Glacier.

The plan was to wake up at midnight and depart for the summit at 1:00am. We would travel in the dark while the snow was the hardest and the snow bridges were still frozen solid. Departing later in the day would risk safely traveling across the glacier.

As planned, we departed the next morning at 1:00am in the pitch darkness. Scott reminded us to "Watch your step," as we left

Trail Tales

the campsite. Watching our step would be tough to do. Even though we were using headlamps, the furthest we could see was five feet in front of us.

When we left Camp Schuman, we were roped together in two teams. We climbed on a smooth snow slope, called The Corridor to 12,000 feet. We took a rest break every hour as we climbed steadily across the heavily crevassed glacier.

Five hours later, the sun was beginning to rise when we reached the first crater. The rim of the crater was snowless with puffs of volcanic steam rising from the cracks in the rim.

Mt Rainier's summit crater rim with puffs of steam melting the snowfield.

With a final push, we crossed a saddle and reached the summit, 14,411 feet- as we walked onto the top, we couldn't imagine a more beautiful, sunny day than this to be on the summit of Mount Rainier.

The summit of Mount Rainier on a sunny July day.

Reaching the summit of any mountain, big or small, is reason to celebrate. We congratulated each other, took some pictures and, after a rest break, began our descent down the mountain.

As we began to descend, Scott yelled out, "Watch your step." We agreed that coming down a mountain could be just as dangerous as ascending. With a sense of purpose, we proceeded with extreme caution!

We reached our campsite 12 hours after we had begun the climb to the top. After a brief rest, we packed our tents and gear and hiked back down to the campground and our cars.

As we hiked down the mountain we passed many climbers heading up the trail with the same excitement and energy a few days before. Excited to be on Mt. Rainier!

Hidden dangers can be closer than you think. Tread lightly.

On Top Of It All

A prairie is a large open area of grassland. A reef is an area of rock, coral or sand just below the surface of a large body of water. Prairie Reef in Montana's Bob Marshall Wilderness Area is neither a prairie nor a reef, but Mike, who is the Prairie Reef Fire Tower Lookout, is on top of it all.

While heading southbound on the Continental Divide Trail (CDT), I heard some interesting stories told by Montana natives about the view from the Prairie Reef Lookout. All said, this short side trail to the lookout would be well worth a detour.

Prairie Reef is the highest point in the Bob Marshall that is accessible by a trail. It is located in the Rocky Mountain Ranger District - Lewis and Clark National Forest. With that distinction, as well as the potential for spectacular scenic views, it was an easy decision to revise my route.

With eight miles to go on the CDT to reach the Benchmark Trailhead and Campground, the side trail to Prairie Reef Lookout was marked with an inconspicuous trail sign pointing the way to the lookout. Making a sharp turn, I began an uphill climb to the tower.

The trail is 4.7 miles long with 3,815 feet of elevation gain. I expected it to be two-hour hike up, but that quickly proved wrong. I was ascending rapidly – trees had shaded the first mile, but the last 3.7 miles were exposed to the hot July sun. As the trail wrapped around the mountain with outstanding views of the Sun River and surrounding wilderness, I soon forgot about the challenging ascent before me.

After two hours of hiking, I realized this was not going to be a "straight-forward" ascent. False summits were everywhere. Just as I was thinking, I was almost at the summit; the trail made a turn and the climb continued. After I passed the saddle, the trail ascended steeply and finally the lookout tower was in view.

At the summit of Prairie Reef is a lookout tower that is manned in the summer months. Of the many lookout towers in the United States, this one ranks near the top in terms of scenic views. The United States Forest Service (USFS) began to use the peak as a lookout in the 1920s, and by 1931, an L-4 cab (cabin) was constructed on the site. The current lookout is an R-6 cab erected in 1968. It stands at an elevation of 8,858 feet on the rocky summit of Prairie Reef.

Trail Tales

Prairie Reef Lookout in the Bob Marshal Wilderness Area

Taking a few minutes to catch my breath and enjoy a water break, I began to notice an individual moving around inside the green tower. Not wanting to barge in on a lookout's home, I slowly circled the perimeter to get closer to the stairs leading to the tower.

The R-6 cab was a wooden outlook house with five steps leading to the porch. The designation R-6 refers to region 6 of the US Forest Service (Washington and Oregon) where the design originated. The roof is flat and extends a few feet beyond the cabin to provide shade. A green wooden porch with a protective railing circles the tower. With a propane tank on one side and ten plastic jerry cans filled with water on the other, the lookout is an all-season home.

"Good afternoon," came a greeting from the front door. "I am Mike, the lookout here at Prairie Reef, come on in and join me."

Mike the Lookout at Prairie Reef.

Trail Tales

Of the over 600 original lookout towers in Montana, about 130 are still standing and approximately 40 are still manned. Many historic towers have been destroyed by fast-moving forest fires or toppled by large windstorms.

Mike arrived by mule in early July and departed by mule after the second snowstorm, which usually occurs in early September. A USFS mule team brought in everything he needed for the summer. Food, water and propane resupplies occurred every two weeks by the same USFS packers that brought him in. Mike stayed on Prairie Reef the entire season. On his "days off" he spent his time exploring the surrounding area.

His primary job was to watch for forest fires in the wilderness and support radio communications for the trail crews and packers operating nearby. Each morning he checked in with the Forest Service's communication center in Great Falls, and each evening checked out. If they failed to hear from him, they would know he may need assistance. He also monitored radio traffic between trail crews to make sure they were safe and not in any danger.

Mike was also a Forest Service public relations representative. He greeted visitors warmly and enjoyed answering every one of their questions. And, Mike loved showing his guests the collection of wildlife pictures he had taken while on the summit – they were nothing short of amazing.

Mike greeting guests at the Prairie Reef Lookout.

Mike's home for the Montana summer was a 15 feet by 15 feet lookout cabin. The structure is fully furnished with a propane stove, propane refrigerator, table, chair, desk and bunk bed around the inside walls. The most important tool that Mike used is in the middle of the lookout, an Osborne Fire Finder.

The Osborne Fire Finder is an alidade, or a turning board, used by lookouts to get a directional bearing on a forest fire. William B. Osborne, a USFS employee created the first Fire Finder in 1915.

The device consists of: a topographic map of the area centered on a horizontal table with a circular rim marked off in degrees. Two sights on opposite sides of the rim are mounted above the map. The sights are used to find coordinates for the location of a fire. When Mike spotted a fire, he radioed a nearby tower and both lookouts then used an intersection method to find the precise location of a fire.

With Mike positioned on top of it all, he was acutely aware of weather patterns especially as the patterns pertain to lightning storms. Lightning strikes are the primary causes of forest fire.

By virtue of the tower's location (high on a rocky peak), the tower itself is at high risk of being struck by lightning. Lightning rods, attached to the roof divert the electrical jolts into the rocks and away from the lookout. His chair and bed sat on glass insulators, offering additional protection during a storm.

Mike proceeded to give me a tour of the lookout and surrounding area. To the west was his outhouse, a rocky-sided open-air structure with an incredible view of the Chinese Wall. To the north and 3,000 feet in the valley below were the remains of a plane crash that occurred years ago. Barely visible to the east was the Benchmark Campground and trailhead. To the south were mountain peaks and a ridgeline with one plume of smoke.

Fire from a lightning strike in the distance.

That smoke was from a fire that started from a lighting strike five days earlier. Mike used his Osborne Fire Finder to spot the fire and report it to the US Forest Service. He was very proud of the fact that he was the first lookout to report it.

With the sun slowly starting to set, it was time for me to depart the Prairie Reef Lookout. I enjoyed the time I spent with him and wealth of information he shared about the life of a fire lookout in Montana.

Mike was on top if it all. He truly loved his job as the lookout at Prairie Reef.

The people you meet can be worth the effort to get there.

The Things They Carried

On every trail maintenance trip I have been on, there is always a wide variety of extra gear, including what many would consider luxury items. A few of these items were:

Pillows – Getting a good night's sleep is important, but pillows still are considered a luxury item. Some individuals carry inflatable pillows, or they bring stuff sacks they can convert to a pillow by stuffing the sacks with clothes. I will never forget a pillow I spotted on a Benton MacKaye Trail trip in Georgia. One of the younger crewmembers brought along a large Sponge Bob pillow. Justin insisted it would help him get a peaceful night's rest.

Guitar and Mandolins – Songs and music are popular evening campfire pastimes. It never ceases to amaze me how crewmembers with a musical gift can play so many songs without music. Brandon, who was on the Appalachian Trail Crew in Maine, was able to make up a song with just a few words of encouragement. His song about Whoopie Pie Dave continues to live on in my mind.

Musical instruments on the trail.

Margaritas – Trail beverages typically are water, tea and coffee. Many crewmembers bring their favorite coffees to enjoy during a cool morning. On a recent Bob Marshall Wilderness Trail trip, Steve and Trish surprised the crew by sharing their margarita mix with everyone – including the salt and limes. The only thing missing was the mariachi band.

Books – Reading material for evening downtimes are very popular. Paperbacks with outdoor themes are the top books that were carried. With the innovation of Kindles and e-books, crewmembers are now able to carry 30 books on a device smaller than one average paperback. Such was the case with Josh who carried a "fully loaded" Kindle on the Alaska climbing trip to the Eldridge Glacier. With what seemed like an unlimited supply of books to read, Josh was the envy of the crew –for the first six days. It was not until the seventh day when Josh learned that sometimes the Kindle is not always better than a paperback. You see paperbacks served two purposes on that six-day Alaska climbing trip that, due to poor weather, was extended to nine days. The first purpose -- reading material while being sequestered in a tent during a bad snowstorm. The second -- toilet paper substitute when supplies ran low. When his supply ran out, Josh had to borrow a few pages from my "Chapter One".

The Beast- Trail maintenance crewmembers typically carry a preferred trail tool on their outings. Tools range from shovels, Pulaskis, trail hoes, axes, rock bars and saws of many types. Phil preferred a unique tool that he called the "Beast" -- a combination of a hoe and axe. If you only had one tool to carry, then the Beast would be it. It can cut roots, clean out water bars, de-berm the edges of a trail and move dirt quickly.

Many varieties of trail tools on the CDT.

Bug Repellants – Bug sprays and liquid repellants are required trail gear, especially during mosquito and black fly seasons. DEET based products have long been the standard repellant, but now new products that include Permethrin, are becoming more prevalent. On a Washington Trail Association log-out, Trent carried an incredibly lightweight Thermocell mosquito repeller that was the envy of the entire crew. Trent had an invisible cloud around him that no mosquito dared enter.

Vintage Crosscut Saws – The crosscut saw of choice on a logout work trip is the Simonds 541. This saw has a perforated lance tooth pattern and can cut trees blocking the trails with ease.

It was in 1834 that Simmons began making saws of various forms and types. Tom, a WTA certified sawyer, carried a vintage Simonds 541 when working on the trails in Washington's Cascade Mountains. Since chain saws were not allowed in wilderness areas, Tom used his crosscut saw to cut out logs on the remote wilderness trails.

Crosscut saw in use in the Washington Cascades.

Bear Spray – In bear country, most tourists visiting national parks will carry bells that make noises to scare the bears away. A majority of trail crewmembers find these jingle bells annoying and useless. If you cross paths with a sow bear and cubs, the bells will not make any difference. Bear spray may give you a fighting chance to escape. I've never met a crewmember who worked in grizzly bear country that didn't carry a can of spray within easy reach if needed. It is better to be safe than sorry

A CDT Hiker with bear spray in easy reach.

The little things in life, the luxury items, are what make the journey enjoyable.

Where To From Here

While the Appalachian Trail (AT) may be the most popular long distance hiking trail in the United States, and the Continental Divide Trail (CDT) one of the longest trails, many new shorter distance trails are being created every year.

Forward-thinking individuals see the need for more trails across public lands. These trails will require trail maintainers to support their efforts.

The tales I've shared with you are just a small portion of the experiences I've had and lessons I've learned.

If trail tales are to continue to be shared and enjoyed, hikers, bikers, climbers and mule riders need to have the opportunity to experience the outdoors, document their experiences and share their tales for future generations.

Acknowledgements

I would like to thank the following individuals for their help over the course of this project.

Emily Cowdrick, for her patience, guidance and encouragement from concept to publication.

Dr. Kara Cowdrick, for her recommendations on the book's theme and content.

Kyle Cowdrick, an adventurer and my companion on many backcountry expeditions.

Martha Williams, for sharing her experiences on publishing and marketing.

Ron and Gail Taylor, for their insight and wisdom on writing a nonfiction book.

My beta readers; Joan Thompson, Tom Martin, and Joe Ochs for their valuable suggestions and guidance.

Joy Forehand, for her editorial suggestions and perseverance with my many updates.

To all of those amazing individuals that I encountered on my backcountry adventures that made Trail Tales possible.

www.ingramcontent.com/pod-product-compliance
Lightning Source LLC
LaVergne TN
LVHW041632070426
835507LV00008B/572